Your Mind Has A Mind Of Its Own

Why Sales Are Never A Good Thing, Why Popcorn Confuses You, And Other Ways Your Brain Is Ruining Your Life

Written & Presented by:

Alex Ogorek

What do you mean "Mind Of Its Own"?

Your brain does a lot of weird stuff. Some of that weird stuff is artsy and cute like product innovation or romantic gestures. But the other weird stuff is... annoying. It makes snap judgements without your consent, it rushes to conclusions based on assumptions, and generally makes your life worse off than if it had done nothing at all.

These faults are collectively known as **cognitive biases.**

And this book is done in a "kinda bad to absolute worst" format, with increasing severity the more you go down it. It covers the 17 *worst* cognitive biases ruining your life and your success, with #1 being the worst of the bunch. (and #17 still being bad, just not *as* bad).

But what even *is* a **cognitive bias**?

They're basically shortcuts and shortcomings that your brain takes/has that clouds its ability to think logically and make rational decisions.

Or, the more detailed description from Wikipedia states:

A **cognitive bias** is a systematic pattern of deviation from norm or rationality in judgment. Individuals create their own "subjective social reality" from their perception of the input. An individual's construction of social reality, not the objective input, may dictate their behaviour in the social world. Thus, cognitive biases may sometimes lead to perceptual distortion, inaccurate judgment, illogical interpretation, or what is broadly called irrationality.

The good news? I'll be giving you tips on how to overcome each one.

So, let's figure out how to fix these, shall we?

But a quick note before we get started...

There are a few other AMAZING books out there that go REALLY deep on some of these (and talk about a LOT MORE than what's covered below).

If this list interests you, I HIGHLY suggest getting these. You can easily follow the links provided and be taken directly to the Amazon listing to buy them there:

Book #1:

You Are Now Less Dumb by David McRaney

https://amzn.to/2HvzREJ

Book #2:

You Are Not So Smart by David McRaney

https://amzn.to/2HuGh6S

Book #3:

The Little Book Of Behavioral Investing by James Montier

https://amzn.to/2Hw266b

Without further ado...

THE LIST!

17. Misinformation Effect

- - - -

What is it:

The **Misinformation Effect** is when your recall of a past event is more "cloudy" and less accurate. Your episodic memory also becomes less easily remembered in detail and more easily affected by outside influencers.

How It's Ruining Your Success:

Ever been to a jury and notice when a witness makes a claim everyone starts believing it more? Or when a person mentions a "blue car" that passed by when in reality it was green. Or was it purple? Ah who cares, the point is that you're being tricked by your own brain into believing false facts, and you're falling right into your own lies.

How to Overcome It:

Sadly, even though it's at the bottom of the list (in terms of severity), this is one of the hardest things to catch, simply because your memories naturally fade with time. Plus, there's evidence showing that every time you recall a memory, you're not recalling the actual event, but instead recalling the last time you recalled the memory. So if someone decides to throw in facts that you're unsure of, try to double check it somehow. Recorded video works best, speaking from experience.

16. Halo Effect / Spillover Effect

- - - -

What is it:

The **Halo Effect**, or sometimes called the **Spillover Effect** is when one or two great qualities or traits about a person, company, location, or object overflows and "spills over" into the other areas, and makes it seem like they're an overall better person, place, or thing than they really are.

How It's Ruining Your Success:

See that cute girl over there? What about that hot guy? That company that always makes great products? Or how about the beach everyone is dying to visit? It's moments like these you'll realize that what you're experiencing is the Halo Effect. Simply having a great attitude and a charming attitude doesn't make smart, or athletic, or good at brushing your teeth every night before going to bed. It just makes you charming with a great attitude. And that company? Well, just because they're good at making 1 great product, doesn't mean they can recreate that success in another domain. If they can, hats off to them! But that's the exception, not the rule. Giving "the benefit of the doubt" or over-weighing subjective circumstances (positively for one person, and negatively for someone else, for example) are other places where the halo effect is the cause.

How to Overcome It:

Yes, that person, place, or thing might truly be talented and gifted in multiple areas of their life. Yes that getaway beach vacation might be full of amazing things to do while you're there. However, even though being great in at least 1 area greatly increases the perception of the rest of the areas, it should be noted that you should (usually) look at each component objectively and in isolation to guarantee you're not being fooled by your own brain.

15. Consistency Bias

- - - -

What is it:

The **Consistency Bias** is when you incorrectly remember your past attitudes and behaviour in order to resemble present attitudes and behaviour. In other words, you think you've always thought the way you do. You think you've always been this conservative. You think you've always been this risk-averse. You think you've always been this open-minded, adventurous, and outgoing. You imagine your previous self as having been like you are today. This stems from the need of the human brain to maintain a sense of identity. If it can't even view itself as being the same over time, how can it trust anything else that appears to be the same over time?

How It's Ruining Your Success:

In reality however, your thoughts, behaviors, moods, attitudes, perspectives, and outlooks on life change and morph over time. When you recall your past self, you imagine a very of the "story" where that person (aka past you) thinks and acts very similarly to how you do today. This ruins your success because you think you've always been this successful, wealthy, outgoing, smart, marketing savvy, interested in new tech (or disinterested in adopting new tech), etc. You imagine your past self as "enlightened" as you journeyed the path forward as if you knew exactly where you were headed in life. Conversely, if you imagine your *future* self, say, 5 years from now, you will imagine yourself as much different, newer, and a changed person compared to what you are now.

How to Overcome It:

Realize that yes, you change over time, and so does everyone else. You are not the same person you were when you were 5, or 18, or 30, or even 65. Nor should you be! You are experiencing life at your own pace and new data points are entering your brain every second. Light photons, sound waves, new technology, social interactions, etc. are all contacting your body every day and making little changes that add up over time.

14. Bandwagon Effect / Groupthink

- - - -

What is it:

The **Bandwagon Effect**, and related **Groupthink**, is when you do something simply because other people are doing it, making it a more attractive option to you than if it were presented by itself. And because other people are doing it, it comes across as "more normal and acceptable", thus prompting you (and everyone else involved) to become more engaged (eg: mob mentality). Here's an example: You like a certain sports team just because they're winning this season, whilst claiming you're a "huge and loyal fan, and always have been" (which is, conveniently, also an example of **Consistency Bias**). Then the next season you come to the "realization" how bad they really are and how lucky they got last season. You're falling into the bandwagon effect.

How It's Ruining Your Success:

If you're the kind of person who thinks like the masses, does things just because they're cool, popular, or trendy, or otherwise engages in activities only because a lot of other people have socially validated that activity, you're limiting yourself much more than you might think is possible. Limiting your mental (and physical) behavior to that which many other people are doing also limits how far you can go. If you want to be like "average Joe", think and act like him.

How to Overcome It:

There's a saying that goes "If you always do what you've always done, you'll always get what you've always got." Aka: Be different, stand out, and become your own person. If you do what every other *ordinary* person is doing (personally and in business), how can you expect *extraordinary* results as an outcome?

13. Pluralistic Ignorance

- - - -

What is it:

Pluralistic Ignorance is when the individuals within a group believe the opposite of what the group as a whole believes. This is sort of related to **Bandwagon Effect** because everyone in the group just goes along with the activity, even thoughts the individuals within the group have conflicting beliefs about the actions. An example being drinking alcohol at a University. Studies have shown that while the perception of drinking is high, in reality most students don't want to get drunk every weekend, and simply put on a show for their friends, partially because they believe their friends want to do that as well. Have you ever found yourself promoting an idea at your workplace or community that everyone seemed to love and also promote, only to find out that nobody liked it in the first place? Then how come nobody spoke up?

How It's Ruining Your Success:

Simply put, if you're simply going along for the ride, everyone loses. You lose because you're doing something you don't want to do or believe. The others lose because they fall victim to this as well, and don't have an example of someone speaking up. And the group / community / workplace / idea loses because it's not being exposed to thoughts that will make it more battle-hardened and resilient for when it's exposed to the public. In all reality, it's counterproductive because it fosters "sameness" as opposed to challenging the belief for the sake of hardening the idea from all angles.

How to Overcome It:

Although much easier said than done, simply tell the truth. Do what *you* want to do. Be honest, open, transparent, and genuine. If you're outspoken about your beliefs, this causes **Pluralistic Ignorance** to go in the positive direction, in that everyone starts sharing their thoughts publicly (because "that's what we do here"), even if they don't personally want to share their thoughts publicly. However, this version of it turns out much more success and positivity than any other form, so I suggest you let it happen.

12. Survivor Bias (Forgotten Failures)

- - - -

What is it:

The **Survivor Bias** is when you only look at the successful outcomes of an activity or group of individual data points. For example, if you only look at the wealthiest people in the world and try to use that data to determine if you should drop out of school (aka, the dropouts that were successful or "survived" the difficulties anyone would face in those circumstances). Or if you're in the military and trying to determine where you should patch up your planes and only look at the bullet holes of the planes that returned to home base (aka, the ones that literally survived and were able to fly home).

How It's Ruining Your Success:

When you only look at a single statistic or data from a single perspective, it's very easy to become biased, then hyped, then immediately let down when it doesn't work in your favor. There's countless examples of being thinking they can make it, but ignored the thousands (or possibly millions) of failures along the way that they never heard about.

How to Overcome It:

This one is actually quite easy to overcome. Simply get more data. If all you're seeing are successful data points, learn more. Try to find counterexamples given the same inputs. For example, if you look at the number of people who used a Keto diet to lose weight, try to find examples of people who *also* used Keto, but where it didn't result in becoming skinny. That way you can prove to yourself there's more to it than "simply doing X".

11. Availability Bias

- - - -

What is it:

The **Availability Bias** is your brain's way of taking information out of context and blowing up the proportions to make it seem more common than it really is. In other words, you believe some things are extremely common (and thus either terrifying you, or are hyping you up, which is sort of like the **Survivor Bias** listed above). The TV and news media outlets are great examples of this. They take very, very uncommon data points and talk about them for daaaays, making it seem like it's happening all the time, everywhere. Same goes for your internal thoughts. Just because you can recall something (aka, is "more available" to your memory), doesn't mean it's any more likely or plausible than stuff you have forgotten.

How It's Ruining Your Success:

What's more common, deaths by shark or deaths by cows? At the rate you hear about shark attacks, you might be surprised to hear more people die from cows every year than die from sharks. Yet it's thoughts like these that ruin your success because you take stuff out of context and forget that life is much more granular, patchy, and rough than a quick simplification and over-generalization of a few data points.

How to Overcome It:

To overcome the **Availability Bias**, you have to be conscious of the fact that all information is not treated equally. Just because something is presented to you, either formally or informally as important or otherwise shocking, does not necessarily mean the data lines up with that. A rather paradoxical example being this thing you're reading now. I've told you these are the 17 worst. But have you ever looked into *all* of the cognitive biases, heuristics, fallacies, or other brain faults you have? Who's to say these are the worst, besides me? Do your own research and figure stuff out for yourself before believing overarching and general statements. NOTHING is just black-and-white. Ever.

10. Illusion of Control

- - - -

What is it:

The **Illusion of Control** happens when you feel like you have control over a situation that you could never possibly change the outcome of. You tend to overestimate your ability to control things that are otherwise immovable and you clearly have no influence over. Have you ever been in a casino and think by waiting until the roulette table turns black 6 times you'll bet on red and win big? Or what about the sports fan that does their pre-game routine with a chant, dance, or other ritual in order to influence the game they're not even playing in? Yup. That's the **Illusion of Control** at work.

How It's Ruining Your Success:

Believing in superstitions, or trying to take action based on a series of false beliefs about your abilities is counterproductive. You are a very confident, optimistic, and delusional to think your skills have anything to do with flipping a coin and trying to predict the outcome, even when the results are rigged and stacked in your favor ahead of time. You might blame yourself for a relationship that went bad, but in reality they had a say in the relationship too!

How to Overcome It:

Thankfully, situations where you don't have control are pretty easy to spot. It might be easier to take correlated data points and assuming causality (eg: thinking you're good at flipping coins or gambling, when you were just getting lucky this entire time). However, it's better for you long-term if you focus on that which you have control over. You do not have control over the stock market, or the game on tv, or even which actor wins an oscar. In a way, you do, but on a scale that's so small and insignificant, it's best left up to chance.

9. Illusion of Transparency

- - - -

What is it:

The **Illusion of Transparency** is when you believe you know what I'm thinking, and simultaneously believe I know what you're thinking. Basically when you're talking to someone, you think it's easy for you (and others) to read minds.

How It's Ruining Your Success:

Any time you're in a debate with someone, or any time you are trying to communicate information to someone, your inability to read people's minds (yet believing you can) leads you to not communicate everything. This leads to confusion, anger, and mistrust in both directions. Ever heard the phrase "Well you should've known what I was going to think"? Or what about those times when you're up on stage giving a speech and all of a sudden you start sweating bullets because you think everyone is judging you and knows how unprepared you are? The truth is, nobody knows. They're just waiting for something to happen, while at the same time too busy thinking about themselves to care about you.

How to Overcome It:

Realize that everyone is selfish. You can never know someone's personal thoughts, only their interpretation of the thoughts as spoken by them. But you can never know them directly (at least not at the time of this writing. Having cool brain-wave reading tech would be totally something to look into). Just take a deep breath and realize that people are not thinking about you, as they cannot understand what's going on in your head. Same goes for communicating with others in an informative matter: Just tell them what they need to know, and stop assuming that they're "picking up the hints", because they're not.

8. Dunning-Kruger Effect

- - - -

What is it:

The **Dunning-Kruger Effect** is your inability to realize, if you're new at something, how unskilled you are. Conversely, it's also your inability to realize, if you're actually good at something and have been doing it for a while, how skilled you actually are, because you understand so many different viewpoints and nuances that it's hard for you to grasp simple concepts within the subject. There are some amazing graphs on the **Dunning-Kruger Effect**, so just googling the term and looking at images will give you a great visual as to what this is.

How It's Ruining Your Success:

When you're brand new to a topic, a sport, a skill, or something that has a lot of nuances, you don't know what you don't know. Therefore when you first start, you think you're picking it up super fast, and think you know *a lot.* There's a joke that an over-confident newbie to a subject is said to be on the peak of "Mt. Stupid" because they believe they're so much better than they actually are. This causes overestimations of skill, and underestimations of time to complete a project.

How to Overcome It:

Just focus on improving your craft every single day. Realize that every topic has experts and you most likely aren't one, especially in the area or subject you just started. Run a bunch of experiments and tests, learn from that data, and keep moving forward. You will eventually get good enough that you'll start learning industry-specific terms. Once you hit that point, it's all about execution (which is what people on the far right side of the skill vs confidence graph have trouble with).

7. Endowment Effect

- - - -

What is it:

The **Endowment Effect** states that you value something more highly if it's something you own. Conversely, you believe other people should value their own items at retail value, and not take the sentimental value into account (when you don't do that yourself). Take for example a cute puppy coffee mug you got as a gift a few years back. If I wanted to buy it off you, you would value the price of the mug *much* higher than the retail value of it simply because there's sentimental value you have personally attached to the object. Another example being the stock market. Every had trouble selling a stock because you're "waiting for it to come back up" before selling? Yup. **Endowment Effect.**

How It's Ruining Your Success:

This ruins your success because you have a viewpoint that's inconsistent with the way the rest of the world views your item or asset. You also start to fall prey to the **Sunk Cost Fallacy** (a bias discussed below), which has compound negative effects on your success. When you overvalue to something simply because you own it, it causes you to undervalue outside situations or assets simply because you *don't* own it. This skews your viewpoint because you are now making it harder on yourself to change and adapt.

How to Overcome It:

This one's tough, but the best approach usually involves getting as many outside opinions as possible. The value in big data vs small data plays out very well here, in the sense that a few individuals have a small percentage chance of being right, but when you gather a large number of data points it's a much higher chance that the group as a whole has the correct result, even if no one individual came to that result.

6. Decoy Effect / Asymmetric Dominance

- - - -

What is it:

The **Decoy Effect** or also called **Asymmetric Dominance** is when 2 items in isolation make you choose the smaller/lesser of the two, and an arbitrary 3rd item is placed in the middle, but priced or otherwise indicated very very closely to the higher/larger of the original two. (Eg: Small, Medium Large popcorn at the movie theaters)

How It's Ruining Your Success:

Marketers loooove this one, because with this bias in your brain, all they need to do is stick a 3rd option somewhere in the middle and it will skew your perspective towards the higher end product almost always. This causes your brain to default to the middle option (because when the Paradox of Choice comes into play, something not discussed here, your brain defaults to the middle before making a decision based on information). After defaulting to the middle, you see the smaller/lower end option as "not worth it" because the middle is placed so closely to the larger/higher end option that you end up choosing the higher end option. *But,* if it were just the lower and higher (and no decoy middle), you would've most likely gone for the lower end. Again with the popcorn example, if it was just Small/Large, you'd go Small. But once they add Medium, you're gravitated towards Large simply because of how close in price/size the Medium is.

How to Overcome It:

This one is very tough to debunk and get around. Luckily there's a few things you can do. First, pay attention to popcorn prices at a movie theater. This is the greatest example of the decoy effect at its finest. If nothing else, go into a theater and notice how your brain wants to subconsciously choose the higher end option just due to "size and price" and "how it just makes sense." This is the **Decoy Effect** at work. Also, any time you're browsing a website and they have a price table, take a very close look at what they're offering with each tier. It's possible that the free, or even bottom tier paid option might be perfectly fine for you, based on the features it offers.

5. Confirmation Bias

- - - -

What is it:

Confirmation Bias is one of the most famous biases out there (in that, more people have heard about this one than probably any others on this list). **Confirmation Bias** is when you only research and agree with the information you already believed in, thereby confirming your beliefs (simultaneously falling prey to the **Consistency Bias** discussed above).

How It's Ruining Your Success:

When you only research things you already believe in, listen to podcasts in audiobooks that talk about the stuff you already believe in, and talk with friends about things you already believe in, you're setting yourself up for a massive failure. **Confirmation Bias** causes you to ignore contradictory evidence, simply because it doesn't jive with what you already believe. If what you believe is actually incorrect, you're going further and deeper in the wrong direction. Health and fitness is a great example of areas where people have conflicting beliefs, and yet everyone is passionate about how correct and perfect their method is compared to others.

How to Overcome It:

Simply realize that not everyone is perfect. Not every opinion matters. Not every person who ever speaks or creates something is a genius or expert in their field. And even if they were, they're probably so deep in the topic that **Confirmation Bias** is strongest from them out of anyone. When doing your own research, make sure to research all sides before making a decision. Weigh your options. Find positive and negative examples. Find counterpoints and counterexamples that could disprove what you're believing to be true. If you're taking disparate and scattered data points and trying to connect them that makes it sound plausible, chances are *very* high that you're falling prey to this bias.

4. Hindsight Bias

- - - -

What is it:

Hindsight Bias is where you think you knew what the end result would be, before the event even took place. For example, let's say there's a football game on TV, Team A vs Team B. At the beginning, you might bet on Team B winning. But at the end of the game, it's "obvious" to everyone why Team B lost the game. Another example: Imagine you hear about someone you know from school, but haven't heard from in a while, shows up in the news as a drug dealer. You might think "Oh I just knew all along that would happen". Every heard the phrase "Hindsight is 20/20"? This is the bias they're talking about.

How It's Ruining Your Success:

When you perceive past events as being obvious and you knowing it the entire time, that gives you a false sense of your (in)ability to predict the future. You can estimate the future, and you can make guesses about what might happen (sometimes with a fairly high degree of accuracy), however you will never be able to truly predict the future. **Hindsight Bias** makes it so that you tie up a story with a nice bow that "makes sense", only after more data points have come in. This leads you to extrapolating future data points and believing you can successfully predict outcomes because you've "successfully predicted" in the past (but you actually haven't).

How to Overcome It:

Although this bias ruins your life pretty substantially, it's thankfully one of the easier ones to overcome. First, you must realize that you didn't "know it all along". Second, you must realize that you can't predict the future. One of the ways to show this to yourself is to write down your predictions, with all the considerations also written down *beforehand*. Then compare these observations and predictions with the actual result, like a scientist following the scientific method (which is why it was created: to overcome this bias).

3. Sunk Cost Fallacy

- - - -

What is it:

The **Sunk Cost Fallacy** is probably something you've heard of before. It's when you continue to put time, energy, money, and effort into a project, relationship, career, or endeavor even when it's clearly obvious to outsiders that the inputs are not worth the outputs. The thinking is that "you've come this far already, can't abandon now or else it'll all be for nothing!". This is the **Sunk Cost Fallacy** at work.

How It's Ruining Your Success:

Whenever you're in a toxic relationship with a significant other, or at a dead-end job that sucks the energy out of you, or working on a project that's costing more and more money and time without any profits or long-term potential (eg: a competitor launches a better product at a lower cost than you planned to sell yours), it's time to move on. Your inability to look at things objectively (similarly tied with the **Endowment Effect** described above) causes you to over-value the effect already invested. That time, energy, money, and effort invested is in the past. You cannot get that back. If you've spent 5 years with someone, or $1 million on a project and it's not turning out the way you hoped, you have to call it quits.

How to Overcome It:

This one is one of the hardest to overcome. Just being honest. However, this change in perspective should change the way you think about your dead-end projects: If you started today, would you continue? If you picked up that relationship from someone else, would you stay? If you inherited that project from another person or company, would you kill it or start working on it? If you detach yourself from *your personal* time invested, it's much easier to realize how silly it is to continue investing into that project, relationship, career, or other endeavor that's not returning the results it needs to.

2. Anchoring Effect

- - - -

What is it:

The **Anchoring Effect** is when you fixate on an initial data point as your point of reference, regardless of where that initial data point came from. For example, ever go into a store that references a $200 pair of jeans for "only $80! 60% Off!"? That's the **Anchoring Effect** coming into play, because your brain was like "I don't know how to price these jeans. They're apparently $80, but is that a good deal? Or is that too expensive?" And unless you have years of experience in the industry to just have a gut feeling of whether something is too high or too low (arguably another form of this bias), you're purely going off the price the company listed as reference, which, to your brain, makes it seem like a good deal, even if that same company paid less than $10 for that pair of jeans to be on that shelf.

How It's Ruining Your Success:

Outside of just pricing concerns (where marketers will play into heavily, because it works), the **Anchoring Effect** can be seen when you compare yourself against other with regards to beauty, success, etc. You can also look up Contrast Bias, which is similar to **Anchoring Effect**, but not discussed here. It ruins you by pushing your emotions around and toying with you, making you feel a lot better or worse than you'd probably normally feel.

How to Overcome It:

Once you realize marketers are just inflating prices so they can "mark them down", and once you realize everybody is on their own path in life, everything will be okay. The best way to overcome this bias is by doing some more research, and shopping around. Make sure you consider all of your options (or at least more than just 1 or 2), and make informed decisions, as opposed to snap judgements or impulse purchases. Sometimes the "value difference" isn't as extreme as they're making it out to be.

1. Learned Helplessness

- - - -

What is it:

Learned Helplessness is when you've given up on life, and given up on trying to do things yourself because you feel like you can't do anything without someone else teaching it to you or you having it handed to you. Okay that's a bit extreme but here are some examples. Dogs in a box they can't escape, shocked, then eventually moved to a box with a door don't leave when shocked. Monkeys in a cage being fed every day by a zookeeper, when let out into the wild don't know how to get food for themselves and die. Humans, who learn by experimentation when they're babies, get "taught" by teachers that the answer is at the back of the book already figured out for them, and it's just about taking more classes from experts to learn more things, as opposed to learning the material and figuring out the problem themselves.

How It's Ruining Your Success:

Learned Helplessness is the #1 item on this list because it's extremely impactful on your ability to move upward in life. It's ruining your relationships. It's ruining your physical health. It's ruining your mental agility and knowledge. It's ruining your career. It's amazing how many areas this 1 bias affects you. Your brain adapts VERY well to its surroundings. So well, in fact, that when your brain is constantly being spoon-fed information as opposed to being forced to go out and learn the information for itself, your brain stops working. It literally shuts down and just accepts the reality that any new information comes in the form of spoon-feeding. Same goes for trust-fund inheritance kids. They (usually) aren't used to the idea of working for money, and instead expect it to just show up whenever they ask mommy or daddy for it. SAME goes for personal and career success. YES it is possible to learn a new skill and a new language and a new area of life. Yet people have been conditioned over their years of schooling and manual labor that the only way to get ahead is by letting someone else do the work for them. This teaches your brain that it's incapable of learning new things, and you give up before you even start, and tell yourself "I'm just not that kind of person." I call bullshit.

1. Learned Helplessness

(cont.)

- - - -

How to Overcome It:

Hands down, the toughest one to overcome. But if you don't take anyway anything else from this list except 1 thing, have it be this: **YOU CAN DO IT.** You have the ability to learn on your own, to grow on your own, and to being the best version of yourself, by yourself. Yes get mentors. Yes get coaches. Yes get guides and tutors and teachers. But **DO NOT** rely on them as a crutch. DO NOT use a lack of one as an excuse to not act. There's always something you can do, at any skill level. And there's always something you can learn, regardless of how much you know or don't know about a topic. It is possible, it is worth it, and I guarantee you, if you stick with it, you'll reap rewards far greater than you ever imagined possible. **Learned Helplessness** is the #1 killer (hence why it's #1 on the list) of pretty much any person going through mainstream society. Traditional school and education killed your creativity. Bosses and dead-end jobs killed your ability to work for yourself. This document. This list. This *movement* is here to make sure you break that spell, chain, and curse. To make sure you rise above and become the greatest version of yourself that you can become, all while putting in the effort and making it happen, as opposed to just waiting for a lucky break. It won't land in your lap. You must reach for it and take it. But like you've read above, you can do it, and it is possible.

And in case you've gained more interest...

I'll say it again here because, honestly, these books are absolutely amazing. There are a few books out there that go REALLY deep on some of these (AND MORE). If this list interests you, I HIGHLY suggest getting these. You can easily follow the links provided and be taken directly to the amazon listing to buy them there:

Book #1:
You Are Now Less Dumb
by David McRaney
https://amzn.to/2HvzREJ

Book #2:

You Are Not So Smart

by David McRaney

https://amzn.to/2HuGh6S

Book #3:

The Little Book Of

Behavioral Investing

by James Montier

https://amzn.to/2Hw266b

BUT! BEFORE YOU GO...

SHARE THIS WITH A FRIEND!

You know they need it.

If you learned something about yourself from this, I'm sure you have someone in your life that would benefit greatly from it as well.

If you ever want to chat or give feedback, you can! Reach out:
www.alexogorek.com

P.S. I want to help you succeed...

If you ever need help with avoiding ANY of the above biases in your own life, I've built the perfect program centered around building lasting life success. Simply visit the following link and you can learn all about the details of what's included:

www.

SevenRulesToSuccess

.com